DK

• MUSIC •
Classical
and Opera

Nicolas Brasch

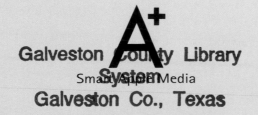

Smart Apple Media

This edition first published in 2005 in the United States of America by Smart Apple Media.

Smart Apple Media
1980 Lookout Drive
North Mankato
Minnesota 56003

Library of Congress Cataloging-in-Publication Data

Brasch, Nicolas.
  Classical music and opera / by Nicolas Brasch.
  p. cm.
  Includes index.
  ISBN 1-58340-547-X (alk. paper)
  1. Music—History and criticism—Juvenile literature. 2. Opera—Juvenile literature. I. Title.

  ML3928.B72 2004
  781.6′8—dc22   2004041453

First Edition
9 8 7 6 5 4 3 2 1

First published in 2003 by
MACMILLAN EDUCATION AUSTRALIA PTY LTD
627 Chapel Street, South Yarra 3141

Associated companies and representatives throughout the world.

Copyright © Nicolas Brasch 2003

Project management by Elm Grove Press
Edited by Helen Duffy
Text design by Judith Summerfeldt Grace
Cover design by Judith Summerfeldt Grace
Photograph research by Helen Duffy and Ingrid Ohlsson

Printed in China

Acknowledgements
The author and the publisher are grateful to the following for permission to reproduce copyright material.

Cover photographs: courtesy of the National Library of Australia (McMurdo, Don, 1930–2001, portrait of Joan Sutherland and Luciano Pavarotti in concert, Sydney Opera House concert hall, 1983, color photograph, 41.2 x 35.5 cm, Don McMurdo performing arts collection [23550014]); Photodisc (musical instruments); Bruce Postle (orchestra).

Text photographs: AKG, London, pp. 12 (Johann Sebastian Bach, composer, Eisenach 21.3.1685 – Leipzig 28.7.1750, portrait, painting, c. 1715, ascribed to Johann Ernst Trensch th.E. Erfurt, Angermuseum), 13 (Wolfgang Amadeus Mozart, composer, Salzburg 27.1.1756 – Vienna 5.12.1791, portrait, painting, 1819, by Barbara Krafft, née Steiner [1764–1825], oil on canvas, 54 x 42 cm [photo: Eric Lessing] Vienna, Gesellschaft der Musikfreunde), 17 (Antonio Vivaldi, violinist and composer, Venice [?] 4.3.1678 – Vienna 28.7.1741, portrait, painting, 1723, by Francois Morellon La Cave, Bologna, Museo Bibliografico Musicale), 18 (Franz Schubert, composer, 1797–1828, *A Schubertiade at Ritter von Spaun's* [Schubert and the singer Johann Michael Vogl at the piano], oil sketch, 1868, by Moritz von Schwind [1804–1871], oil on canvas, 23 x 18 cm, Vienna, Hist. Museum der Stadt Wien), 22 (Josef Haydn, composer, 1732–1809, scenery of the first performance of *L'incontro improviso* at the private theater of the Esterhazy palace in 1775 [front left the composer at the harpsichord], gouache with ivory, Munich, Deutsches Theatermuseum); Brand X Pictures, p. 1 (sheet music); Grand Hotel et de Milan archives, p. 27; courtesy of the National Library of Australia, pp. 3 (second bottom, McMurdo, Don, 1930–2001, portrait of Victoria Vergara as Carmen, the Australian Opera, June 1991, picture/negative, Don McMurdo performing arts collection [23366378]), 3 (bottom, McMurdo, Don, 1930–2001, Australian Opera performance of *Otello*, starring Joan Carden as Desdemona and Kenneth Collins as Otello, August 1996, Don McMurdo performing arts collection [23406818]), 14 (Annois, Len, 1906–1966, sketch for *Swan Lake* [194-?], drawing, pastel on board, 38.2 x 56 cm, Geoffrey Ingram Archive of Australian Ballet [21735930]), 19 (Stringer, Walter, 1907–2001, Australian Ballet performance of *The Sleeping Beauty*, starring Maina Gielgud and Gary Norman, 1974, color photograph, 25 x 20 cm, in W. F. Stringer collection of dance photographs [24092750]), 20 (McMurdo, Don, 1930–2001, portrait of Victoria Vergara as Carmen, the Australian Opera, June 1991, picture/negative, Don McMurdo performing arts collection [23366378]), 21, 24 (McMurdo, Don, 1930–2001, Australian Opera performance of *Otello*, starring Joan Carden as Desdemona and Kenneth Collins as Otello, August 1996, Don McMurdo performing arts collection [23406818]), 25 (McMurdo, Don, 1930–2001, portrait of David Hobson as Ferrando and Jeffrey Black as Guglielmo, dressed as Albanians, in *Cosi fan tutte*, the Australian Opera, June 1990, color photograph/negative, Don McMurdo performing arts collection [23371531]), 26 (McMurdo, Don, 1930–2001, portrait of Joan Sutherland and Luciano Pavarotti in concert, Sydney Opera House concert hall, 1983, color photograph, 41.2 x 35.5 cm, Don McMurdo performing arts collection [23550014]), 28 (McMurdo, Don, 1930–2001, Australian Opera Performance of *Aida*, starring Greg Scott as Pharaoh, Bernadette Cullen as Amneris, and Horst Hoffman as Radamès, July 1995, picture/negative, Don McMurdo performing arts collection [23334400]), 30 (McMurdo, Don, 1930–2001, Australian Opera performance of *Carmen* starring Victoria Vergara as Carmen, June 1991, picture/negative, Don McMurdo performing arts collection [23366320]; Photodisc (musical instruments), pp. 7, 8, 9, 10, 11; Bruce Postle, pp. 1 (left, classical violinist), 1 (right, David Helfgott performing at Spray Farm, Victoria), 3 (top), 4 (from the collection in the Louvre, Paris), 5, 15, 29.

While every care has been taken to trace and acknowledge copyright, the publisher tenders their apologies for any accidental infringement where copyright has proved untraceable. Where the attempt has been unsuccessful, the publisher welcomes information that would redress the situation.

Contents

Glossary
When a word is printed in **bold** you can find its meaning in the Glossary on page 31.

Understanding Music

Music has been enjoyed since ancient times.

Main Elements of Music

The main elements of all music are:

dynamics the variation in volume (from loud to soft)

pitch the depth of a sound (whether it is "high" or "low")

rhythm the general pattern or movement of a piece of music, which is created by the length of time between each beat

timbre the tonal quality of a sound

tonality the use of keys in music

Important Musical Terms

chord a combination of two or more musical notes played at the same time

harmony a specific chord or a series of chords

melody a series of musical sounds of different pitch (when you hum the tune of a song, you are usually humming the melody)

texture the thickness of a sound

Music is the arrangement and performance of a combination of sounds that are created by the human voice or by instruments. The ability to turn sounds into music or to create sounds that do not come naturally is something that only humans can do.

The desire to make music is common among all people. It helps us to communicate ideas or emotions and to understand our surroundings and way of life, as well as that of others.

Since ancient times, even isolated communities developed their own forms of music. Different groups used different techniques and instruments to create their own musical sounds.

Music is a creative art form. It also plays an important role in other art forms. Dance and some forms of theater use music to support the action on stage and to help create mood. Music also helps to create atmosphere in films and many television programs.

Music has its own written language, or **score**, made up of symbols and notes. Different musical notes are used to indicate the length of a sound. Notes are represented by the letters A, B, C, D, E, F, and G. These letters or notes are marked on a stave, which is a set of five parallel lines. The position of a note on the stave indicates whether the note is high or low.

Some of the most well-known types of music are:

- classical
- opera
- jazz
- blues
- folk
- country
- reggae
- pop
- rock

This book is about classical music and opera.

Classical Music

The term "classical music" refers to music that is serious and expected to last for generations. The term also refers to a particular historical period from the mid-1700s to the early 1800s.

Classical music follows rules of style and rhythm and often takes a traditional form, such as a sonata, symphony, or concerto. The serious and timeless character of classical music makes it different from simpler and more widely popular music, such as pop, rock, and folk music. These forms of music are seen as less serious, less worthy, and not as long-lasting.

Writing Classical Music

Early classical composers wrote music for several reasons:

- to worship God
- to please the ruler of a particular state or country
- to celebrate an important event

Music inspired by religion was generally performed in a church or cathedral as part of a religious occasion.

It was also common for rulers to employ court musicians and composers. The composers were expected to write pieces of music to mark particular occasions or to impress important visitors.

Performing Classical Music

Classical music today is usually written for performance in a concert hall, church, or opera house. Audiences listen, rather than dance to the music. Classical music is often played by an **orchestra**, but is also performed by smaller groups of **instrumentalists** or a single musician.

History of Classical Music

Great Composers of the Medieval Period

Léonin (c. 1163–1201) French

Philippe de Vitry (1291–1361) French

Guillaume de Machaut (c. 1300–1377) French

John Dunstable (c. 1390–1453) English

Guillaume Dufay (c. 1398–1474) French

Gilles de Bins dit Binchois (c. 1400–1460) Franco-Flemish

Great Composers of the Renaissance Period

Josquin Desprez (c. 1440–1521) French

Thomas Tallis (c. 1505–1585) English

Giovanni da Palestrina (c. 1525–1594) Italian

William Byrd (1543–1623) English

Thomas Morley (c. 1557–1602) English

The timeline illustrates the seven time periods in classical music and lists the main instruments of each period. Different colours have been used to represent the different time periods.

Classical music is divided into seven time periods: Early Music, Medieval, Renaissance, Baroque, Classical, Romantic, and Modern.

Early Music

Early Music was the first major period in the history of music. It dated from about A.D. 600 to about A.D. 1100. Voices, rather than instruments were used to make music. The most popular form of singing was chanting. Gregorian **chants**, named after Pope Gregory I, were pieces of music sung in churches and cathedrals by monks.

Medieval

The Medieval period (also known as the Middle Ages) dated from the 1100s to the 1400s. People sang with very little backing from musical instruments. A **vocal** style developed called **polyphony**, meaning music for many voices.

Renaissance

The Renaissance period dated from the 1400s to the early 1600s. It was a time when people were making great discoveries about the world in which they lived. Renaissance music began in Italy and made greater use of harmony. The madrigal, a song for five or six voices, was performed without any instrumental **accompaniment**, or backing. The **lyrics**, or words, were often about love. During this period, music was also written for dancing.

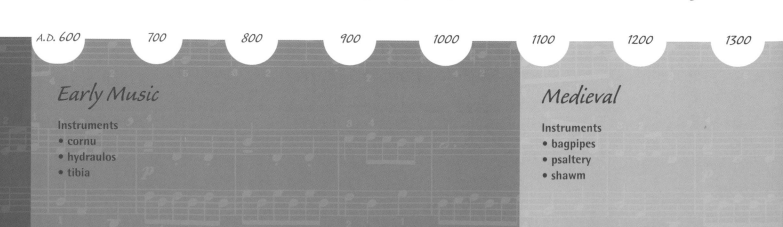

A.D. 600　　700　　800　　900　　1000　　1100　　1200　　1300

Early Music

Instruments
- cornu
- hydraulos
- tibia

Medieval

Instruments
- bagpipes
- psaltery
- shawm

Baroque

The Baroque period dated from the early 1600s to the mid-1700s. "Baroque" was originally a term used to describe the ornate architecture of this time. The decorations and flourishes that were visible in the architecture could also be seen in the music. The use of harmony became even more complex and composers started using a technique called **counterpoint**.

The lute was often used in Renaissance music.

Classical

The Classical period dated from the mid-1700s to the early 1800s. Composers paid far more attention to the structure of a piece of music than earlier composers. Everything had to be in exactly the right place and follow certain rules.

Romantic

In the Romantic period, from the early 1800s to the early 1900s, composers used their work to express their emotions. They let their imaginations run wild. Orchestras that play romantic music are usually very large, often with as many as 100 players.

Clarinet

Modern

The Modern period in music refers to the past 100 years. The type of music in this period varies far more than in any other period. Modern music is characterized by **experimentation** and it often ignores some of the strict rules of the past. Modern composers have experimented or taken risks with different musical sounds. They get inspiration from all sorts of sources. Some modern pieces even include sounds from objects such as typewriters, vacuum cleaners, and computers.

The piccolo (above) and the clarinet were often used in Romantic music.

1400	1500	1600	1700	1800	1900	2000

Renaissance		Baroque	Classical	Romantic	Modern
Instruments		Instruments	Instruments	Instruments	Instruments
• cittern	• lute	• harpsichord	• flute	• clarinet	• cymbals
• clavichord	• viol	• mandolin	• piano	• guitar	• piano
• crumhorn		• Oboe d'Amore	• violin	• piccolo	• synthesizer
		• violin			

Instruments of the Orchestra

There are four main sections to an orchestra. They are string, woodwind, brass, and percussion.

Role of the Conductor

An orchestra is led by a conductor, who has many roles, both before and during a performance. He or she often plans the entire season for a musical company, then organizes and runs rehearsals. During a performance, the conductor stands on a raised platform in front of the orchestra to conduct, and uses a small stick, called a baton, to make sure the musicians follow the written music, or score, properly.

The String Section

The main string instruments are the violin, viola, cello, and double bass. The harp also features in some orchestras.

The violin and viola are four-stringed instruments that are held under the player's chin. They are played by drawing a **bow** across the strings The viola is slightly bigger than the violin and has a duller, deeper sound.

The cello and double bass are like big violins. The cello is played sitting down, while the double bass can be played sitting down or standing up. The musician draws the bow across and in front of their body. The cello has a very rich sound, while the double bass has a lower sound than the other string instruments.

The harp is a very old instrument, dating back to around 2200 B.C. The modern double-action pedal harp has 47 strings. The pedals are used to alter the pitch.

Cello

Harp

The Woodwind Section

The most popular woodwind instruments are the flutes, oboe, clarinet, and bassoon.

The three types of flute are the flute, alto flute, and piccolo. They are the only woodwind instruments that require the musician to blow across a hole, rather than straight into the hole. They are held sideways from the mouth. Most modern flutes are made from metal rather than wood.

The flute is 26 inches (67 cm) long and has 13 sound holes and 16 keys. The keys open and close the sound holes. The alto flute is 11 inches (29 cm) longer than a flute and produces a deeper sound. It is sometimes referred to as the bass flute. The piccolo is the smallest of the three flutes. It is 13 inches (33 cm) long and produces higher sounds than the other flutes.

The oboe is a **reed instrument**. The "reed" is a small piece of cane or metal, which is attached to the mouth of the instrument to change the sound. The oboe has a double reed, with a piece of cane split in two and folded over. The instrument is about 26 inches (65 cm) long and has a slight pear-shaped end. It produces a smooth sound that can be dulled for effect by putting a handkerchief in the end. There is a longer type of oboe called a cor anglais. It produces a deeper sound.

The clarinet is also a reed instrument. It is a similar shape to the oboe, but is slightly longer and has a larger opening at its end. Another difference is that clarinet players blow into a single reed, rather than a double reed. The clarinet produces a wider range of notes than the oboe.

The bassoon has a double reed and features a curved metal crook, known as a bocal, which enables the instrument to be held away from the body.

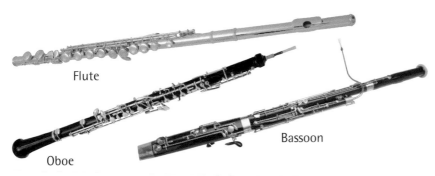

Flute

Oboe

Bassoon

Performers of Classical Music

Apart from an orchestra, other performers of classical music are:

- **ensemble** a group of two or more musicians or singers who each play an equal role
- **quartet** a group of four musicians (the most common form of quartet is a string quartet, which comprises two violins, one viola, and a cello)
- **soloist** a single performer
- **trio** a group of three musicians playing the same or different instruments (which may include the voice).

World-famous Orchestras

The date in brackets refers to the year in which the orchestra was founded.

Vienna Philharmonic Orchestra (1842) Austria
Boston Symphony Orchestra (1881) United States
Berlin Philharmonic Orchestra (1882) Germany
Chicago Symphony Orchestra (1891) United States
St. Petersburg Philharmonic Orchestra (1921) Russia
New York Philharmonic Symphony Orchestra (1842) United States
Sydney Symphony Orchestra (1934) Australia
Israel Philharmonic Orchestra (1936) Israel
Royal Philharmonic Orchestra (1946) England

The Brass Section

The main brass instruments are the French horn, trumpet, cornet, trombone, and tuba.

The French horn has the appearance of a tube coiled around and around. The sound comes out of a wide bell, behind the player. The sound can be regulated by pressing various valves and by the amount of pressure put on the mouthpiece. The sound can pass through more than 16 feet (5 m) of brass tubing before being released.

The sound from the trumpet comes out in front of the musician. The trumpet has three valves that regulate how much tubing the sound travels through, which determines the pitch of the sound produced.

As the trumpet can make a louder sound than any other instrument in the orchestra, it is often fitted with a mute. A mute is a cone-shaped object that reduces the volume of the instrument.

The cornet is shaped and played like a trumpet but is slightly smaller. It produces a sound that has similarities with both the trumpet and the French horn.

The trombone is different from the trumpet and cornet because it has a **slide**. Moving the slide regulates the distance the sound travels, and this determines the pitch of the sound. The slide can be moved to any one of seven positions. The lowest note is produced when the slide is extended all the way out.

The tuba is the largest brass instrument. Its large bell helps produce very deep, low sounds, which come out above the musician's head.

French horn

Trumpet, fitted with a mute

Tuba

Trombone

The Percussion Section

There are many different percussion instruments. Anything that makes a loud banging or crashing sound can be used. Modern composers have even written parts for whips, sirens, and typewriters. However, the most common percussion instruments are the timpani, bass drum, snare drum, cymbals, triangle, tambourine, and xylophone.

The timpani is also known as the kettledrum. It is shaped like a large cooking cauldron and has a skin stretched tightly over the top. Sound is produced by hitting the skin with sticks. The sticks are covered at one end with a material such as felt, wood, or sponge. The type of material used determines the sound that comes out.

The bass drum is a large drum that stands on its side and can be hit on either of its two heads. The stick used to hit the drum usually has a tip made from felt. Sometimes, a wire brush is used instead of a stick to produce a metallic sound.

Like the bass drum, the snare drum has two heads. However, it stands upright on a stand and only one of the heads is struck with a stick. The bottom head has wires stretched across it and these vibrate to produce a rattling sound when the top head is struck.

Cymbals are plate-shaped instruments made from brass. They are struck against each other to produce a clashing sound. Often cymbals are suspended on a stand and struck with a stick or wire brush.

The tambourine is a small, hand-held drum. It has spaces along the side containing small brass disks, like mini cymbals. These jingle when the tambourine is shaken or hit, usually with a part of the musician's hand.

The triangle is a triangular-shaped piece of steel. It is suspended from a piece of string and hit with a metal rod.

The xylophone has wooden keys arranged like piano keys. Sound is produced by hitting the keys with a small **mallet**. The end of the mallet that makes contact with the keys is usually made of rubber, metal, or wood.

Timpani drum (the pedal is used to change the pitch)

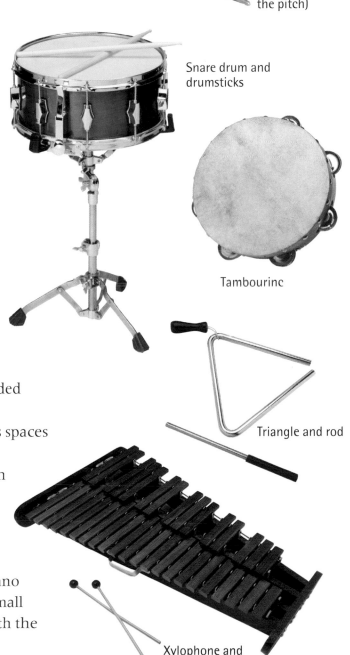

Snare drum and drumsticks

Tambourine

Triangle and rod

Xylophone and wooden mallets

Great Classical Composers

Other Great Composers of the Baroque Period

Claudio Monteverdi (1567–1643) Italian
Henry Purcell (1659–1695) English
Georg Telemann (1681–1767) German
Jean-Philippe Rameau (1683–1764) French

Composers are people who write pieces of music. They are influenced by the times they live in and the instruments available.

George Frideric Handel

Born February 23, 1685, Halle, Germany (died 1759)
Music period Baroque
Compositions include *Music for the Royal Fireworks* (suite), *Water Music* (suite), *Messiah* (oratorio)
Profile Handel's father at first refused to let his son play music, but finally agreed. The young Handel spent several years studying and composing in Italy before moving to England. He is best known for his oratorios.

Antonio Vivaldi

Born March 4, 1678, Venice, Italy (died 1741)
Music period Baroque
Compositions include *Four Seasons* (concerto), *Ottone in Villa* (opera), *The Faithful Shepherd* (concerto)
Profile Vivaldi trained as a priest before learning the violin. He began teaching and composing in his early twenties and became known throughout Europe for his performances and compositions. He is most famous for his violin concertos.

Johann Sebastian Bach

Johann Sebastian Bach

Born March 21, 1685, Eisenach, Germany (died 1750)
Music period Baroque
Compositions include *St. Matthew Passion* (passion), *Brandenburg Concertos* (six concertos for strings and wind instruments), *The Art of Fugue* (fugue)
Profile Bach came from a very musical family. He played the organ in church before becoming a teacher and composer. Of all the classical composers, Bach's works are among the most passionate and emotional.

Wolfgang Amadeus Mozart

Born January 27, 1756, Salzburg, Austria
(died 1791)
Music period Classical
Compositions include *Requiem* (requiem),
The Magic Flute (opera), *Symphony No. 41* (symphony)
Profile Mozart was a child genius who composed
complicated pieces of music at the age of five. He
worked as a court composer, then as a teacher and
private composer. He included musical elements
that had not been used before.

Franz Peter Schubert

Born January 31, 1797, Vienna, Austria (died 1828)
Music periods Classical and Romantic
Compositions include *Unfinished Symphony* (symphony),
"Great" C Major Symphony (symphony)
Profile Schubert showed musical talent early in life.
He composed many different styles of music, but is
best known for his lieder, which are songs written
for one voice and piano.

Ludwig van Beethoven

Born December 1770, Bonn, Germany (died 1827)
Music period Classical
Compositions include *Symphony No. 5* (symphony),
Symphony No. 9 (symphony), *Violin Concerto in
D Major* (concerto)
Profile Beethoven's father and grandfather were
musicians. From his mid-twenties, Beethoven
gradually became deaf. Even when he was totally
deaf, he continued composing, imagining the sounds
in his head. He is best known for his symphonies.

Wolfgang Amadeus Mozart

Other Great Composers of the Classical Period

Thomas Arne (1710–1778) English
Christoph Gluck (1714–1787) Bohemian–German
Johann Stamitz (1717–1757) Bohemian
Joseph Haydn (1732–1809) Austrian
Johann Christian Bach (1735–1782) German
Luigi Boccherini (1743–1805) Italian
Antonio Salieri (1750–1825) Italian

More Great Classical Composers

Other Great Composers of the Romantic Period

Nicolò Paganini (1782–1840) Italian
Carl Maria von Weber (1786–1826) German
Hector Berlioz (1803–1869) French
Franz Liszt (1811–1886) Hungarian

Fryderyk Franciszek Chopin

Born March 1810, Zelazowa Wola, Poland (died 1849)
Music period Romantic
Compositions include *Piano Sonata in C minor* (sonata), *Là ci Darem Variations* (piece for piano and orchestra), *Fantasie in F minor* (solo piano piece)
Profile Chopin began piano lessons at the age of seven and composing lessons at the age of 12. He moved to Paris in 1831, where he became a leading composer of his time. He is most famous for his compositions for piano.

Pyotr Il'yich Tchaikovsky

Born May 7, 1840, Kamsko-Votkinsk, Russia (died 1893)
Music period Romantic
Compositions include *The Nutcracker* (ballet), *Swan Lake* (ballet), *1812 Overture* (overture)
Profile Tchaikovsky studied law before becoming a music teacher and composer. He greatly admired Mozart and included elements of Mozart's work in his own. Tchaikovsky's ballets are particularly famous and are among the most performed ballets in the world.

Gustav Mahler

Born July 7, 1860, Kaliste, Bohemia (died 1911)
Music period Romantic
Compositions include *Das Lied von der Erde* (**song cycle**), *Symphony No. 1* (symphony), *Symphony No. 2* (symphony)
Profile Mahler studied the piano and composition before earning a living as a conductor. He was as well known as a conductor as he was as a composer. His compositions combined elements of modern classical music and earlier musical forms.

Australian artist Len Annois made this sketch for a production set of Tchaikovsky's ballet *Swan Lake*.

Igor Stravinsky

Born June 17, 1882, Lomonosov, Russia (died 1971)
Music period Modern
Compositions include *The Rite of Spring* (ballet),
The Firebird (ballet), *The Rake's Progress* (opera)
Profile Stravinsky's father was an opera singer and his
mother was a pianist. Stravinsky studied law before
becoming a composer. In 1913, *The Rite of Spring* caused a
riot among the Russian audience, who were shocked at
Stravinsky's modern style of music.

Other Great Composers of the Modern Period

Béla Bartók (1881-1945) Hungarian
Alban Berg (1885-1935) Austrian
John Cage (1912–1992) American
Pierre Boulez (born in 1925) French
Peter Sculthorpe (born in 1929) Australian
Philip Glass (born in 1937) American

Dmitry Shostakovich

Born September 25, 1906, St. Petersburg, Russia (died
1975)
Music period Modern
Compositions include *Symphony No. 7* (symphony), *The Lady
Macbeth of the Mtsensk District* (opera), *Bright Stream* (ballet)
Profile Shostakovich's mother was a professional pianist
who gave him his first music lessons. He composed his first
symphony while a student and was seen at once as one of
the world's most promising composers. Throughout his
career, his music was closely linked to his belief in
communism, the system of government in his homeland.

Leonard Bernstein

Born August 25, 1918,
Massachusetts, United States
(died 1990)
Music period Modern
Compositions include *West Side Story*
(musical), *Symphony No. 1: Jeremiah*
(symphony)
Profile Bernstein's father bought
his son a piano when he was ten,
and the boy began lessons.
He became a famous conductor,
pianist, and composer. Many of his
compositions combined classical
music with jazz and pop.

Leonard Bernstein's musical *West Side Story* is considered a modern opera.

Great Classical Compositions

Major Types of Classical Composition

ballet music music written to accompany a ballet performance

cantata vocal work for a chorus, but usually with some sections for solo voices

chamber music music written for a small group of musicians

choral work music written for a large number of voices

concerto music written for a single instrument backed by an orchestra

duet music for two instruments, which may be the same or different instruments

fugue composition for voices, in which the voices enter at different times

lied German song, written for one voice and a piano

mass religious passages set to music

opera a stage drama set to music

oratorio religious text set to music for voice and instruments

overture music written for an orchestral introduction to a major work, but can become a work in its own right

passion musical piece describing the crucifixion of Christ

requiem musical setting of the mass for the dead

sonata music for one or two instruments, generally in three movements

string quartet music written for two violins, a viola, and a cello

suite music for dance movements

symphony music written in four movements for a large group of players

A composition is a piece of music. There are many different types of classical compositions.

Beethoven's *Symphony No. 9*

Year completed 1824
Composer Ludwig van Beethoven
Type of work symphony
This symphony is one of the most famous ever composed. It was unlike any symphony written before because it featured a choir and **solo** voices in the final movement, which was called "Ode to Joy."

Mozart's *Symphony No. 41*

Year completed 1788
Composer Wolfgang Amadeus Mozart
Type of work symphony
Also known as the *Jupiter Symphony*, this was one of three symphonies that Mozart wrote in six weeks.

Mendelssohn's *Symphony No. 4*

Year completed 1833
Composer Felix Mendelssohn
Type of work symphony
This work is also known as Mendelssohn's "Italian Symphony" because he wrote it after traveling through Italy. It captures the color and beauty of the Italian countryside.

Vivaldi's *Four Seasons*

Year completed c. 1725
Composer Antonio Vivaldi
Type of work concerto
Four Seasons is four concertos, written for a violin and orchestra. Each concerto represents one of the four seasons and the music progresses from the lightness of spring to the harshness of winter.

Rakhmaninov's *Piano Concerto No. 2*

Year completed 1901
Composer Sergey Rakhmaninov
Type of work concerto
Most orchestras around the world have performed this classic concerto. While writing it, the composer suffered from severe depression and was cured by a hypnotist. Rakhmaninov dedicated the concerto to him in gratitude.

Antonio Vivaldi

Beethoven's *Sonata in A Major*

Year completed 1803
Composer Ludwig van Beethoven
Type of work sonata
This sonata for violin and piano is also known as the "Kreutzer Sonata" as Beethoven dedicated it to French violinist Rodolphe Kreutzer (1766–1831).

Schubert's *Piano Sonata in B Flat*

Year completed 1828
Composer Franz Peter Schubert
Type of work sonata
This was the last of 21 piano sonatas that Schubert wrote and was published after his death. It is one of the most performed piano pieces in the world.

More Great Classical Compositions

Tchaikovsky's *1812 Overture*

Year completed 1880
Composer Pyotr Il'yich Tchaikovsky
Type of work orchestral overture
This was written by Tchaikovsky in memory of Russia's military defeat of France in 1812. It is a rousing piece of music that features bells and the use of percussion instruments to sound like cannon fire.

Brahms' *Tragic Overture*

Year completed 1886
Composer Johannes Brahms
Type of work orchestral overture
This is one of only two overtures written by Brahms. The other was the *Academic Festival Overture* (1880). Brahms said of his two overtures, "one weeps, the other laughs."

Schubert's *String Quartet No. 14*

Year completed 1824
Composer Franz Peter Schubert
Type of work string quartet
Also titled *Death and the Maiden*, this music used elements from a song of the same name that Schubert had written in 1819. It is a bleak, dark piece of music, composed just four years before the composer died.

An artist's sketch shows composer Franz Schubert and singer Johann Vogl at the piano during a private musical evening.

Handel's *Messiah*

Year completed 1742
Composer George Frideric Handel
Type of work oratorio
This is a piece of music for voices and orchestra and it celebrates the life, death, and resurrection of Jesus Christ. It is one of the best-known pieces of classical music.

Verdi's *Requiem*

Year completed 1874
Composer Giuseppe Verdi
Type of work choral work
This was written in honor of a famous Italian writer named Alessandro Manzoni.

The Sleeping Beauty

First performed 1890
Composer Pyotr Il'yich Tchaikovsky
Type of work ballet music
This was first performed as a ballet in January 1890 at the Mariinsky Theatre in St. Petersburg in Russia. *The Sleeping Beauty* follows the story of the famous fairy tale of the same name.

The Rite of Spring

First performed 1913
Composer Igor Stravinsky
Type of work ballet music
The Rite of Spring was originally written for a ballet but later became a concert piece. When it was first performed, the use of pounding rhythms and extreme force were unlike anything the audience had heard before.

Peter and the Wolf

First performed 1936
Composer Sergey Prokofiev
Type of work classical music for children
This music tells the story of several characters, which are represented by different instruments. Peter is represented by the string instruments. The Wolf is represented by the French horns, the Grandfather by the bassoons, the Bird by the flutes, the Duck by the oboes, the Cat by the clarinets, and the Hunters by the percussion section.

Tchaikovsky's *Sleeping Beauty* is a frequently performed ballet. This is a scene from an Australian Ballet production that starred Maina Gielgud and Gary Norman.

Other Great Ballets

Giselle (1841) Adolphe Adam
Swan Lake (1877) Pyotr Il'yich Tchaikovsky
The Firebird (1910) Igor Stravinsky

Opera

Opera is a stage production in which the characters tell the story by singing. The music is played by an orchestra and is a major feature. It includes **arias** and **choruses**. Opera singers need some acting ability but it is the quality of their voice that is most important.

Main Features of Opera

There are two main aspects to an opera, the words and the music. The words, which are known as the **libretto**, are put to music and sung. Most composers of opera write the music and a **librettist** writes the words. However, some composers also write the words.

Modern opera performances usually feature a big cast of characters, elaborate costumes and **sets**, and special lighting and sound effects. They are generally staged in large, specially designed opera houses.

Types of Opera

There are two main types of opera, comic opera and dramatic opera. The main aim of a comic opera is to make people laugh. The main aim of a dramatic opera is to give the audience an emotional experience, and storylines are usually tragic, with one or more popular characters dying.

Some operas are referred to as "grand" operas. These are large-scale, serious operas that generally have a story based on historical events. Operas with very simple storylines and uncomplicated music are called "operettas."

The Structure of Opera

Operas consist of an overture, followed by several acts. The overture is a piece of music that is played before the opera begins. It sets the mood for what is to follow.

The acts of an opera are like the acts in a stage play or the chapters of a book. A change of act often means a change in location and scenery. Most operas have three acts, but some have four or five.

The Cast of an Opera Production

Putting on an opera is a massive effort. It involves people doing many different jobs. Among the people required are:

- singers who have lead roles
- singers who have main parts but not the lead roles
- singers who make up the chorus
- a conductor who leads the orchestra
- members of the orchestra who play the music
- a stage manager who makes sure everything runs smoothly
- a director who works out how the opera will be staged
- a set designer who designs the sets or background scenery
- set builders who build the sets
- a costume designer who designs the costumes
- costume makers who make the costumes
- a lighting designer who works out where all the stage lights will be placed
- technicians who operate the lights and move the sets during the performance

Dame Nellie Melba was an Australian opera performer who was known worldwide for her great singing voice.

Range of Voices

Opera performers are categorized according to their voice range. The voice range from highest to lowest is:

FEMALE VOICE

- soprano
- mezzo-soprano
- contralto

MALE VOICE

- tenor
- baritone
- bass

History of Opera

The first performance of *L'incontro improviso*, an opera by Josef Haydn, was held in a private theater of the Esterhazy palace in 1775. The composer is on the left, playing the **harpsichord.**

In the late 1500s, some men in Florence, Italy, decided to stage a play based on ancient Greek drama. They believed that the Greeks had sung, rather than spoken, their words. The Italians wrote *Dafne*, which had its **premiere** in 1597. It was the world's first opera.

The 1600s

In the early 1600s, most operas were performed privately in the houses of the rich and famous. Composers were paid to write operas for special occasions. In 1637, the first public performance of an opera took place in the Italian city of Venice. After this, opera became a public entertainment. By 1700, arias were a common feature of opera.

The 1700s

By the early 1700s, opera in Italy had become so popular that there were ten opera houses in Venice alone. Italian opera usually involved conflict and misunderstanding, then a happy ending. Opera soon spread across Europe.

1597
Premiere of *Dafne*, the first opera to be performed

1607
Premiere of Claudio Monteverdi's *L'Orfeo*, the first opera to make extensive use of melody

1672
Premiere of Jean-Baptiste Lully's *Les fêtes de l'Amour et de Bacchus* marks the beginning of French opera

1689
Premiere of Henry Purcell's *Dido and Aeneas* marks the beginning of British opera

1728
Premiere of John Gay's *The Beggar's Opera*, one of the first examples of musical comedy

1762
Premiere of *Orfeo ed Euridice* by Christoph Gluck, whose operas brought music and drama closer together

1769
Premiere of Wolfgang Mozart's first opera, *La finta semplice*

1791
Premiere of Wolfgang Mozart's final opera, *The Magic Flute*

1500s

1600s

1700s

French opera developed its own style. It was more serious than Italian opera. The French also developed a lighter form of opera, *opéra comique*, in which some of the words were spoken rather than sung. In England, opera audiences preferred light, amusing operas.

One feature of opera in the 1700s was the popularity of castratos. These were male sopranos or contraltos. Their high range was a result of having their testicles cut off while they were boys, before their voice broke.

The 1800s

During the early 1800s, the main feature of opera was bel canto, or beautiful singing. Italian operas, in particular, highlighted the range and beauty of the human voice. By the mid-1800s, grand opera had become popular, with massive sets and huge casts. Austrian and German opera developed, following the Italian style. Two opera composers were dominant, the Italian Giuseppe Verdi, and the German Richard Wagner. In England, Gilbert and Sullivan were popular with their light, musical comedies.

The 1900s

With tension between European countries before World War I, the theme of many operas was nationalism. The music was stirring and the words were serious. From the 1920s onward, opera composers began experimenting with musical techniques. Some did away with melody, others brought in elements of jazz and, later, rock music.

Great Opera Houses of the World

The date refers to the year when the opera house held its first performance.

Théâtre National de l'Opéra (1672)
Paris, France
Opéra-Comique (1715) Paris, France
Covent Garden (1735) London, England
La Scala (1778) Milan, Italy
Teatro la Fenice (1792) Venice, Italy
Mariinsky Theatre (1860) St. Petersburg, Russia
Vienna Staatsoper (1869) Vienna, Austria
Metropolitan Opera House (1883) New York, United States
Glyndebourne (1934) Glyndebourne, Sussex, England
Sydney Opera House (1973) Sydney, Australia

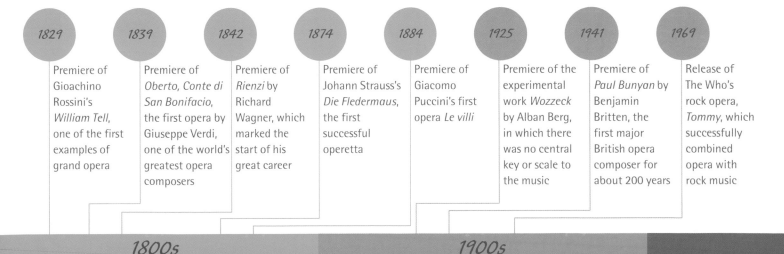

1829
Premiere of Gioachino Rossini's *William Tell*, one of the first examples of grand opera

1839
Premiere of *Oberto, Conte di San Bonifacio*, the first opera by Giuseppe Verdi, one of the world's greatest opera composers

1842
Premiere of *Rienzi* by Richard Wagner, which marked the start of his great career

1874
Premiere of Johann Strauss's *Die Fledermaus*, the first successful operetta

1884
Premiere of Giacomo Puccini's first opera *Le villi*

1925
Premiere of the experimental work *Wozzeck* by Alban Berg, in which there was no central key or scale to the music

1941
Premiere of *Paul Bunyan* by Benjamin Britten, the first major British opera composer for about 200 years

1969
Release of The Who's rock opera, *Tommy*, which successfully combined opera with rock music

1800s   1900s

Great Opera Composers

Other Great Opera Composers

ITALIAN COMPOSERS

Claudio Monteverdi (1567–1643)

Francesco Cavalli (1602–1676)

Gaetano Donizetti (1797–1848)

Vincenzo Bellini (1801–1835)

Pietro Mascagni (1863–1945)

Luigi Dallapiccola (1904–1975)

FRENCH COMPOSERS

Jean-Baptiste Lully (1632–1687)

Jean-Philippe Rameau (1683–1764)

Hector Berlioz (1803–1869)

Georges Bizet (1838–1875)

Claude Debussy (1862–1918)

Alban Berg (1885–1935)

Opera composers write the music to an opera and librettists write the words. Some composers do both. They also have to write for performers with different voice ranges as well as for various instruments.

Giuseppe Verdi

Born October 9 or 10, 1813, Roncole, Italy (died 1901)

Music period Romantic

Operas include *La traviata, Rigoletto, Aida*

Profile Verdi learned the organ, studied composing, and wrote his first opera in 1836. He is considered the greatest of the Italian opera composers.

Giacomo Puccini

Born December 22, 1858, Lucca, Italy (died 1924)

Music period Romantic

Operas include *La bohème, Tosca, Madama Butterfly*

Profile Puccini came from a family of professional musicians. He was an **organist**, then became a composer after seeing a performance of Verdi's *Aida*. Puccini later took over from Verdi as the most popular Italian opera composer.

Gioachino Rossini

Born February 29, 1792, Pesaro, Italy (died 1868)

Music period Romantic

Operas include *The Barber of Seville, Otello, William Tell*

Profile Rossini's parents were musicians and he learned the violin and horn. He began composing in his teens, then worked as a professional singer before returning to composing.

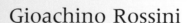

Rossini's opera *Otello* is loosely based on Shakespeare's play *Othello*. This scene shows Joan Carden as Desdemona and Kenneth Collins as Otello.

Wolfgang Amadeus Mozart

Born January 27, 1756, Salzburg, Austria (died 1791)
Music period Classical
Operas include *The Magic Flute, Don Giovanni, The Marriage of Figaro, Cosi fan tutte*
Profile Mozart, a child genius, composed many different types of music. His early operas followed the Italian tradition, while his later operas were more German in style. His operas are among those most performed today.

Richard Wagner

Born May 22, 1813, Leipzig, Germany (died 1883)
Music period Romantic
Operas include *Tristan and Isolde, The Flying Dutchman, The Ring of the Nibelung* (consisting of four full-length operas)
Profile Wagner grew up in a non-musical family but became interested in music at school, then studied it at college. He worked as a conductor while trying to make his name as a composer. His *Ring of the Nibelung* is considered one of the greatest operas.

Opera productions often require colorful and elaborate costumes and sets. This scene from Mozart's *Cosi fan tutte* shows David Hobson as Ferrando and Jeffrey Black as Guglielmo, dressed as Albanians.

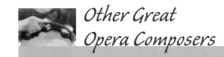
Other Great Opera Composers

AUSTRIAN AND GERMAN COMPOSERS
George Frideric Handel (1685–1759)
Christoph Gluck (1714–1787)
Joseph Haydn (1732–1809)
Richard Strauss (1864–1949)
Kurt Weill (1900–1950)

BRITISH COMPOSERS
Henry Purcell (1659–1695)
John Gay (1685–1732)
Sir Arthur Sullivan (1842–1900)
Ralph Vaughan Williams (1872–1958)
Gustav Holst (1874–1934)

Benjamin Britten

Born November 22, 1913, Lowestoft, England (died 1976)
Music period Modern
Operas include *A Midsummer Night's Dream, Peter Grimes, The Turn of the Screw*
Profile Britten's mother encouraged his love of music. He studied piano before becoming a professional composer. He wrote classical music of various forms before turning to opera.

Great Opera Performers

Most leading female roles in operas are for sopranos and most leading male roles are for tenors.

Dame Nellie Melba

Born May 19, 1861, Melbourne, Australia (died 1931)
Major roles Gilda in *Rigoletto* (Verdi), Mimi in *La bohème* (Puccini), Marguerite in *Faust* (Gounod)
Profile Music was an important part of Melba's upbringing. She made her opera **debut** in 1884, in Melbourne, then traveled to London where she established herself as a leading soprano of the time.

Maria Callas

Born December 2 or 4, 1923, New York, United States (died 1977)
Major roles Aida in *Aida* (Verdi), Lucia in *Lucia di Lammermoor* (Donizetti), Tosca in *Tosca* (Puccini)
Profile Callas's family migrated from Greece to the United States before she was born, but she studied singing in Greece as a teenager. She made her professional opera debut in 1941, and became a great soprano of the time.

Dame Joan Sutherland

Born November 7, 1926, Sydney, Australia
Major roles Lucia in *Lucia di Lammermoor* (Donizetti), Alcina in *Alcina* (Handel), Marguerite in *Faust* (Gounod)
Profile Sutherland's mother was a singer and encouraged her to learn the piano and train as a singer. Sutherland won the *Sun* Aria singing competition in 1949, then moved to London. By 1960, she had established herself as one of the great modern sopranos.

Dame Joan Sutherland and Luciano Pavarotti appeared together in concert at the Sydney Opera House concert hall in 1983.

Enrico Caruso

Born February 27, 1873, Naples, Italy (died 1921)
Major roles Radamès in *Aida* (Verdi), Dick Johnson in *La fanciulla del West* (Puccini), Duke of Mantua in *Rigoletto* (Verdi)
Profile Caruso's mother encouraged him to follow a musical career. He performed in cathedrals before his opera debut in Naples in 1894. Within five years, he was hailed as one of the greatest tenors of all time.

Enrico Caruso is splendidly dressed for a 1914 performance of *Un ballo in maschera*, an opera by Giuseppe Verdi.

Luciano Pavarotti

Born October 12, 1935, Modena, Italy
Major roles Alfredo in *La traviata* (Verdi), Tonio in *The Daughter of the Regiment* (Donizetti), Rodolfo in *La bohème* (Puccini)
Profile Pavarotti's father was a baker who enjoyed choir singing, and his son joined the same choir. Pavarotti won the Achille Peri prize for singing in 1961, and made his opera debut later that year. He gained international fame after appearing several times with Dame Joan Sutherland.

Placido Domingo

Born January 21, 1941, Madrid, Spain
Major roles Siegmund in *The Valkyrie* (Wagner), Otello in *Otello* (Verdi), Alfredo in *La traviata* (Verdi)
Profile Domingo grew up in Mexico, where he studied music and performed in his parents' music company. His first major opera role was in Mexico City in 1961. In the 1980s, he won fame as one of "The Three Tenors," alongside Pavarotti and José Carreras.

Other Great Opera Performers

MALE OPERA PERFORMERS

Farinelli (1705–1782) Italian soprano castrato
Jussi Björling (1911–1960) Swedish tenor
Tito Gobbi (1913–1984) Italian baritone
Mario Lanza (1921–1959) American tenor
Franco Corelli (born in 1921) Italian tenor
José Carreras (born in 1946) Spanish tenor
Andrea Bocelli (born in 1958) Italian tenor
Bryn Terfel (born in 1965) Welsh baritone

FEMALE OPERA PERFORMERS

Marian Anderson (1902–1993) American contralto
Dame Janet Baker (born in 1933) English mezzo-soprano
Montserrat Caballé (born in 1933) Spanish soprano
Marilyn Horne (born in 1934) American mezzo-soprano
Mirella Freni (born in 1935) Italian soprano
Hildegard Behrens (born in 1937) German soprano
Dame Kiri Te Kanawa (born in 1944) New Zealand soprano
Cecilia Bartoli (born in 1966) Italian mezzo-soprano

Great Operas

Other Great Italian Operas

L'Orfeo (1607) Claudio Monteverdi

Lucia di Lammermoor (1835)
   Gaetano Donizetti

The Daughter of the Regiment (1840)
   Gaetano Donizetti

Rigoletto (1851) Giuseppe Verdi

La traviata (1853) Giuseppe Verdi

La bohème (1896) Giacomo Puccini

Italian opera often has a story of unfulfilled love. Austrian and German opera is often based on fairy tales and supernatural happenings. French opera is often grand opera, *opéra comique* (the words are spoken as well as sung) or opéra-ballet, which includes dancing as well as singing.

Aida

Composer Giuseppe Verdi
Librettist Antonio Ghislanzoni
First performed December 24, 1871, Cairo, Egypt
Type of opera grand opera
Main characters Aida (soprano), Radamès (tenor), Amneris (mezzo-soprano), Amonasro (baritone)
Story line Set in ancient Egypt, an Egyptian soldier falls in love with the daughter of the King of Ethiopia, with whom Egypt is at war. The lovers try to run away together but their plan is discovered.

The Barber of Seville

Composer Gioachino Rossini
Librettist Cesare Sterbini
First performed February 20, 1816, Rome, Italy
Type of opera comic opera
Main characters Rosina (mezza-soprano), Almaviva (tenor), Figaro (baritone), Basilio (bass), Bartolo (baritone)
Story line Set in Seville, Italy, in the 1700s, an old man and a young man fight to win the love of a young woman.

Madama Butterfly

Composer Giacomo Puccini
Librettists Giuseppe Giacosa and Luigi Illica
First performed February 17, 1904, Milan, Italy
Type of opera dramatic opera
Main characters Cio-Cio-San or Madama Butterfly (soprano), B. F. Pinkerton (tenor), Sharpless (baritone)
Story line Set in Nagasaki, Japan, in the early 1900s, an American sailor marries a Japanese woman but then deserts her.

A lavish Australian Opera production of Verdi's *Aida* starred Greg Scott as Pharaoh, Bernadette Cullen as Amneris and Horst Hoffman as Radamès.

The Magic Flute

Composer Wolfgang Amadeus Mozart
Librettist Emanuel Schikaneder
First performed September 30, 1791,
Vienna, Austria
Type of opera comic fairy tale
Main characters Tamino (tenor), Pamina
(soprano), Sarastro (bass), Papageno
(bass-baritone)
Story line Tamino, a prince, is given a magic
flute to protect him from a serpent.
Tamino is then sent on a mission to save a
princess from the clutches of an evil priest.
In the end, good triumphs over evil.

Other Great German and Austrian Operas

Tamerlano (1724) George Frideric Handel
Orfeo ed Euridice (1762) Christoph Willibald Gluck
The Marriage of Figaro (1786) Wolfgang Amadeus Mozart
Elektra (1909) Richard Strauss
The Threepenny Opera (1928) Kurt Weill

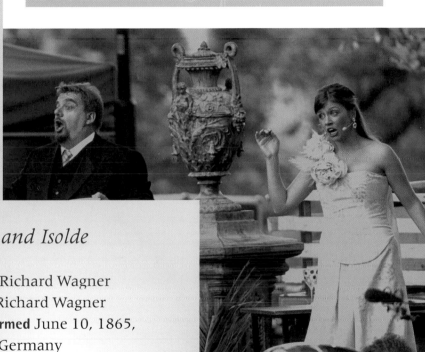

The Ring of the Nibelung

Composer Richard Wagner
Librettist Richard Wagner
First performed August 13–17,
1876, Bayreuth, Germany
Type of opera dramatic opera
Main characters Wotan
(bass-baritone), Alberich
(bass-baritone), Freia (soprano),
Siegmund (tenor), Brünnhilde
(soprano), Sieglinde (soprano),
Siegfried (tenor)
Story line *The Ring* is four operas:
*The Rhinegold, The Valkyrie,
Siegfried* and *Twilight of the Gods*.
Set on the Rhine River, it is a
fairy tale with supernatural
elements. The cycle is usually
performed over three days.

Tristan and Isolde

Composer Richard Wagner
Librettist Richard Wagner
First performed June 10, 1865,
Munich, Germany
Type of opera dramatic opera
Main characters Tristan (tenor), Isolde
(soprano), King Marke (bass),
Brangäne (soprano), Kurwenal
(baritone), Melot (tenor)
Story line Set on board a ship and
then in England, Isolde and Tristan
are in love, even though Isolde is
married to Tristan's uncle, King
Marke. They secretly meet but are
found out.

Modern opera performances are sometimes held away from opera houses, such as in
parks and gardens, to appeal to a wide audience.

More Great Operas

Carmen

Composer Georges Bizet
Librettists Henri Meilhac and Ludovic Halévy
First performed March 3, 1875, Paris, France
Type of opera *opéra comique*
Main characters Carmen (mezzo-soprano), Don José (tenor), Escamillo (baritone)
Story line Set in Seville, Spain, about 1830, a soldier, Don José, falls in love with Carmen, a gypsy. When Don José finds out that Carmen has been seeing a bullfighter named Escamillo, Don José kills Carmen.

An Australian Opera production of *Carmen* starred Victoria Vergara as Carmen.

Other Great Operas

Porgy and Bess (1935) George Gershwin
War and Peace (1946) Sergey Prokofiev
The Rake's Progress (1951) Igor Stravinsky
Einstein on the Beach (1976) Philip Glass and Robert Wilson

The Trojans

Composer Hector Berlioz
Librettist Hector Berlioz
First performed November 4, 1863, Paris, France
Type of opera dramatic opera
Main characters Cassandra (mezzo-soprano), Aeneas (tenor), Corebus (baritone)
Story line Set in ancient Troy, this is based on a story, *The Aeneid*, by Virgil, which describes the battles between the Greeks and the Trojans.

Peter Grimes

Composer Benjamin Britten
Librettist Montagu Slater
First performed June 7, 1945, London, England
Type of opera dramatic opera
Main characters Peter Grimes (tenor), Ellen Orford (soprano), Captain Balstrode (baritone), Mrs Sedley (mezzo-soprano)
Story line Set in an English coastal town, fisherman Peter Grimes is told not to hire another young fisherman, following the death at sea of a boy he had employed. However, Peter Grimes ignores the order and hires another boy. When this boy dies, Peter Grimes sets sail, sinks his boat and drowns himself.

Glossary

accompaniment   support or backing provided by instruments (or voices)

aria   song in an opera that is sung by one performer (usually with a complicated melody)

bow   wooden stick with horse's hair stretched along its length

chants   songs, usually with religious meaning, in which several syllables or words are sung to the same note

chorus   group of singers who back up the solo performers

counterpoint   the art of combining different melodies, or a number of instrumental voices in musical layers, in a single piece of music

debut   first public appearance on a stage

experimentation   trying something new or different

harpsichord   stringed keyboard instrument similar to a piano, but the keys are plucked rather than struck

instrumentalists   people who play instruments

librettist   someone who writes the words to an opera

libretto   words of an opera

lyrics   words to a song

mallet   hammer-like tool with a head made of rubber, metal, or wood

orchestra   large group of people playing different types of instruments, usually string, woodwind, brass, and percussion

organist   someone who plays the organ

polyphony   music for two or more voices, each with their own melody, but all singing in harmony

premiere   first performance

reed instrument   instrument with a mouthpiece made of cane or metal, which vibrates when blown into (in some instruments, such as the accordion and concertina, the reed is operated by air blown from a bellows)

score   written copy of a piece of music

set   the background scenery used to represent particular locations in a stage production, such as a ballet or opera

slide   the part of the trombone that is operated by a musician sliding their arm backward and forward, and which alters the pitch

solo   one single performer, or instrument, playing on its own

song cycle   series of songs with a common theme

vocal   singing style

Index